Santa's
Favorite Cookies
Sweet Treats for the Christmas Season

PUBLICATIONS INTERNATIONAL, LTD.

Microwave Cooking: Microwave ovens vary in wattage. Use the cooking times as guidelines and check for doneness before adding more time.

Santa's Favorite Cookies

Sweet Treats for the Christmas Season

Brownies & Bars

Mystical Layered Bars

⅓ **cup margarine or butter**
1 **cup graham cracker crumbs**
½ **cup old-fashioned or quick oats**
1 **can (14 ounces) sweetened condensed milk**
1 **cup flaked coconut**
¾ **cup semisweet chocolate chips**
¾ **cup raisins**
1 **cup coarsely chopped pecans**

Preheat oven to 350°F. Melt margarine in 13×9-inch baking pan. Remove from oven. Sprinkle graham cracker crumbs and oats evenly over margarine; press down with fork. Drizzle condensed milk over oats. Layer coconut, chocolate chips, raisins and pecans over milk. Bake 25 to 30 minutes or until lightly browned. Cool in pan on wire rack 5 minutes. Cut into bars; cool completely. *Makes 3 dozen bars*

Praline Brownies

Brownies

- 1 package DUNCAN HINES® Chocolate Lovers'
  Milk Chocolate Chunk Brownie Mix
- 2 eggs
- 1/3 cup water
- 1/3 cup canola oil plus additional for greasing
- 3/4 cup chopped pecans

Topping

- 3/4 cup firmly packed brown sugar
- 3/4 cup chopped pecans
- 1/4 cup butter or margarine, melted
- 2 tablespoons milk
- 1/2 teaspoon vanilla extract

1. Preheat oven to 350°F. Grease 9-inch square pan.

2. For brownies, combine brownie mix, eggs, water, oil and 3/4 cup pecans in large bowl. Stir with spoon until well blended, about 50 strokes. Spread in prepared pan. Bake at 350°F for 35 to 40 minutes. Remove from oven.

3. For topping, combine brown sugar, 3/4 cup pecans, melted butter, milk and vanilla extract in medium bowl. Stir with spoon until well blended. Spread over hot brownies. Return to oven. Bake for 15 minutes longer or until topping is set. Cool completely in pan on wire rack. Cut into bars.

Makes about 16 brownies

Chocolate Peanut Bars

- 1/2 cup butter or margarine, softened
- 1/4 cup granulated sugar
- 1 cup packed brown sugar, divided
- 2 eggs, separated
- 1 teaspoon vanilla
- 2 cups all-purpose flour
- 2 teaspoons baking powder
- 1/2 teaspoon baking soda
- 1/4 teaspoon salt
- 2 to 4 tablespoons milk
- 1 cup (6 ounces) semisweet chocolate chips
- 3/4 cup salted peanuts, coarsely chopped

Preheat oven to 350°F. Lightly grease a 13×9-inch pan. Beat butter, granulated sugar and 1/4 cup of brown sugar in large bowl. Beat in egg yolks and vanilla. Combine flour, baking powder, baking soda and salt in small bowl. Blend into butter mixture. Stir in enough milk to make a smooth, light dough. Press on bottom of prepared pan. Sprinkle chocolate chips over top; press lightly into dough. Beat egg whites in large bowl until stiff, but not dry. Gradually beat in remaining 3/4 cup brown sugar. Spread mixture evenly over dough in pan; top with peanuts. Bake 25 to 30 minutes or until top is puffed, lightly browned and feels dry. Cut into 2×1-inch bars while still warm.

Makes about 5 dozen bars

Praline Brownies

Luscious Lemon Bars

Grated peel from 2 lemons
2 cups all-purpose flour
1 cup butter
½ cup powdered sugar
¼ teaspoon salt
1 cup granulated sugar
3 eggs
⅓ cup fresh lemon juice
Powdered sugar

1. Preheat oven to 350°F. Grease 13×9-inch baking pan; set aside. Place 1 teaspoon lemon peel, flour, butter, powdered sugar and salt in food processor. Process until mixture forms coarse crumbs.

2. Press mixture evenly into prepared 13×9-inch baking pan. Bake 18 to 20 minutes or until golden brown.

3. Beat 3 teaspoons lemon peel, granulated sugar, eggs and lemon juice in medium bowl with electric mixer at medium speed until well blended.

4. Pour mixture evenly over warm crust. Return to oven; bake 18 to 20 minutes or until center is set and edges are golden brown. Remove pan to wire rack; cool completely.

5. Dust with powdered sugar; cut into 2×1½-inch bars. Do not freeze. *Makes 3 dozen bars*

Decadent Brownies

½ cup dark corn syrup
½ cup butter or margarine
6 squares (1 ounce *each*) semisweet chocolate
¾ cup sugar
3 eggs
1 cup all-purpose flour
1 cup chopped walnuts
1 teaspoon vanilla
Fudge Glaze (recipe follows)

Preheat oven to 350°F. Grease 8-inch square pan. Combine corn syrup, butter and chocolate in large heavy saucepan. Place over low heat; stir until chocolate is melted and ingredients are blended. Remove from heat; blend in sugar. Stir in eggs, flour, chopped walnuts and vanilla. Spread batter evenly in prepared pan. Bake 20 to 25 minutes or just until center is set. *Do not overbake.* Meanwhile, prepare Fudge Glaze. Remove brownies from oven. Immediately spread glaze evenly over hot brownies. Cool in pan on wire rack. Cut into 2-inch squares.

Makes 16 brownies

Fudge Glaze

3 squares (1 ounce *each*) semisweet chocolate
2 tablespoons dark corn syrup
1 tablespoon butter or margarine
1 teaspoon light cream or milk

Combine chocolate, corn syrup and butter in small heavy saucepan. Stir over low heat until smooth; add cream.

Luscious Lemon Bars

Caramel Fudge Brownies

    1 jar (12 ounces) hot caramel ice cream
       topping
 1¼ cups all-purpose flour, divided
    ¼ teaspoon baking powder
       Dash salt
    4 squares (1 ounce *each*) unsweetened
       chocolate, coarsely chopped
    ¾ cup butter or margarine
    2 cups sugar
    3 eggs
    2 teaspoons vanilla
    ¾ cup semisweet chocolate chips
    ¾ cup chopped pecans

Preheat oven to 350°F. Lightly grease 13×9-inch baking pan.

Mix topping and ¼ cup flour in bowl; set aside.

Combine remaining 1 cup flour, baking powder and salt in small bowl; mix well.

Place unsweetened chocolate squares and butter in medium microwavable bowl. Microwave at HIGH 2 minutes or until butter is melted; stir until smooth.

Stir sugar into melted chocolate. Add eggs and vanilla; stir until combined.

Add flour mixture, stirring until well blended. Spread chocolate mixture evenly into prepared pan.

Bake 25 minutes. Immediately after removing brownies from oven, spread caramel mixture over brownies. Sprinkle top with chocolate chips and pecans.

Return pan to oven; bake 20 to 25 minutes or until topping is golden brown and bubbling. *Do not overbake.* Cool brownies completely in pan on wire rack. Cut into 2×1½-inch bars.

Makes 3 dozen brownies

Almond Toffee Bars

    ¾ cup butter or margarine, softened
    ¾ cup packed brown sugar
 1½ cups all-purpose flour
    ½ teaspoon almond extract
    ½ teaspoon vanilla extract
    ¼ teaspoon salt
    1 package (6 ounces) semi-sweet real
       chocolate pieces
    ¾ cup BLUE DIAMOND® Chopped Natural
       Almonds, toasted

Preheat oven to 350°F. Cream butter and sugar; blend in flour. Add extracts and salt, mixing well. Spread in bottom of ungreased 13×9×2-inch baking pan. Bake in 350°F oven 15 to 20 minutes or until deep golden brown. Remove from oven and sprinkle with chocolate pieces. When chocolate has melted, spread evenly; sprinkle with almonds. Cut into bars; cool.

Makes about 40 bars

Caramel Fudge Brownies

Yuletide Linzer Bars

1⅓ cups butter or margarine, softened
¾ cup sugar
1 egg
1 teaspoon grated lemon peel
2½ cups all-purpose flour
1½ cups whole almonds, ground
1 teaspoon ground cinnamon
¾ cup raspberry preserves
Powdered sugar

Preheat oven to 350°F. Lightly grease 13×9-inch baking pan.

Beat butter and sugar in large bowl with electric mixer until creamy. Beat in egg and lemon peel until blended. Mix in flour, almonds and cinnamon until well blended.

Press 2 cups dough into bottom of prepared pan. Spread preserves over crust. Press remaining dough, a small amount at a time, evenly over preserves.

Bake 35 to 40 minutes until golden brown. Cool in pan on wire rack. Sprinkle with powdered sugar; cut into bars. *Makes 36 bars*

Black Russian Brownies

4 squares (1 ounce each) unsweetened chocolate
1 cup butter
¾ teaspoon ground black pepper
4 eggs, lightly beaten
1½ cups granulated sugar
1½ teaspoons vanilla
⅓ cup KAHLÚA® Liqueur
2 tablespoons vodka
1⅓ cups all-purpose flour
½ teaspoon salt
¼ teaspoon baking powder
1 cup chopped walnuts or toasted sliced almonds
Powdered sugar (optional)

Preheat oven to 350°F. Line bottom of 13×9-inch baking pan with waxed paper. Melt chocolate and butter with pepper in small saucepan over low heat, stirring until smooth. Remove from heat; cool.

Combine eggs, granulated sugar and vanilla in large bowl; beat well. Stir in cooled chocolate mixture, Kahlúa and vodka. Combine flour, salt and baking powder; add to chocolate mixture and stir until blended. Add walnuts. Spread evenly in prepared pan.

Bake just until wooden toothpick inserted into center comes out clean, about 25 minutes. *Do not overbake.* Cool in pan on wire rack. Cut into bars. Sprinkle with powdered sugar.
Makes about 2½ dozen brownies

Yuletide Linzer Bars

Crimson Ribbon Bars

6 tablespoons butter or margarine, softened
½ cup firmly packed brown sugar
1 teaspoon vanilla
½ cup all-purpose flour
¼ teaspoon baking soda
1½ cups old-fashioned oats
1 cup chopped walnuts
½ cup chopped BLUE RIBBON® Calimyrna or Mission Figs
⅓ cup SMUCKER'S® Red Raspberry Preserves

Heat oven to 375°F. Combine butter, brown sugar and vanilla; beat until well blended. Add flour and baking soda; mix well. Stir in oats and walnuts. Reserve ¾ cup mixture for topping. Press remaining oat mixture into 8-inch square baking pan. Combine figs and preserves; spread mixture to within ½ inch of edges. Sprinkle with reserved oat mixture; press lightly. Bake 25 to 30 minutes or until golden brown. Cool in pan; cut into bars. *Makes 20 bars*

Preparation Time: 20 minutes

Cook Time: 25 minutes

Total Time: 45 minutes

Supreme Chocolate Saucepan Brownies

1 cup butter or margarine
2 cups sugar
1/2 cup HERSHEY'S Cocoa
4 eggs, beaten
⅔ cup all-purpose flour
½ teaspoon salt
¼ teaspoon baking soda
2 teaspoons vanilla extract
2 cups (12-ounce package) HERSHEY'S Semi-Sweet Chocolate Chips
½ cup macadamia nuts, coarsely chopped

1. Heat oven to 350°F. Grease 13×9×2-inch baking pan.

2. Melt butter in medium saucepan over low heat. Add sugar and cocoa; stir to blend. Remove from heat. Stir in eggs. Stir together flour, salt and baking soda; stir into chocolate mixture. Stir in vanilla, chocolate chips and nuts. Spread in prepared pan.

3. Bake 30 to 35 minutes or until brownies begin to pull away from sides of pan and begin to crack slightly; *do not underbake*. Cool completely; cut into bars. *Makes about 24 brownies*

Crimson Ribbon Bars

Triple Chocolate Brownies

3 squares (1 ounce *each*) unsweetened chocolate, coarsely chopped
2 squares (1 ounce *each*) semisweet chocolate, coarsely chopped
½ cup butter
1 cup all-purpose flour
½ teaspoon salt
¼ teaspoon baking powder
1½ cups sugar
3 eggs
1 teaspoon vanilla
¼ cup sour cream
½ cup milk chocolate chips
   Powdered sugar (optional)

Preheat oven to 350°F. Lightly grease 13×9-inch baking pan.

Place both chocolates and butter in microwavable bowl. Microwave at HIGH 2 minutes or until butter is melted; stir until smooth. Cool to room temperature.

Combine flour, salt and baking powder in small bowl.

Beat sugar, eggs and vanilla in large bowl until slightly thickened. Beat in chocolate mixture until well combined. Add flour mixture; beat until blended. Add sour cream; beat until combined. Stir in chocolate chips. Spread mixture evenly into prepared pan.

Bake 20 to 25 minutes or until toothpick inserted into center comes out almost clean. *Do not overbake.* Cool brownies completely in pan on wire rack. Cut into 2-inch squares. Sprinkle with powdered sugar, if desired. *Makes 2 dozen brownies*

Marshmallow Krispie Bars

1 package DUNCAN HINES® Fudge Brownie Mix, Family Size
1 package (10½ ounces) miniature marshmallows
1½ cups semi-sweet chocolate chips
1 cup creamy peanut butter
1 tablespoon butter or margarine
1½ cups crisp rice cereal

1. Preheat oven to 350°F. Grease bottom of 13×9-inch pan.

2. Prepare and bake brownies following package directions for basic recipe. Remove from oven. Sprinkle marshmallows on hot brownies. Return to oven. Bake for 3 minutes longer.

3. Place chocolate chips, peanut butter and butter in medium saucepan. Cook over low heat, stirring constantly, until chips are melted. Add rice cereal; mix well. Spread mixture over marshmallow layer. Refrigerate until chilled. Cut into bars.
Makes about 2 dozen bars

Tip: For a special presentation, cut cookies into diamond shapes.

Triple Chocolate Brownies

Cookie Jar Classics

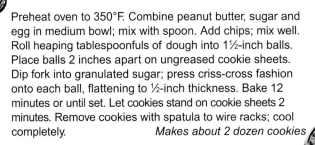

Peanut Butter Chocolate Chippers

1 cup creamy peanut butter
1 cup packed light brown sugar
1 egg
¾ cup milk chocolate chips
Granulated sugar

Preheat oven to 350°F. Combine peanut butter, sugar and egg in medium bowl; mix with spoon. Add chips; mix well. Roll heaping tablespoonfuls of dough into 1½-inch balls. Place balls 2 inches apart on ungreased cookie sheets. Dip fork into granulated sugar; press criss-cross fashion onto each ball, flattening to ½-inch thickness. Bake 12 minutes or until set. Let cookies stand on cookie sheets 2 minutes. Remove cookies with spatula to wire racks; cool completely.   *Makes about 2 dozen cookies*

Chocolate Chips Thumbprint Cookies

1 cup HERSHEY₀S Semi-Sweet Chocolate
   Chips, divided
½ cup sugar
¼ cup butter flavor shortening
¼ cup (½ stick) butter or margarine, softened
1 egg, separated
½ teaspoon vanilla extract
1 cup all-purpose flour
¼ teaspoon salt
1 cup finely chopped nuts

1. Heat oven to 350°F. Lightly grease cookie sheet. Place ¼ cup chocolate chips in small microwave-safe bowl. Microwave at HIGH (100%) 20 to 30 seconds or just until chocolate is melted and smooth when stirred; set aside to cool slightly.

2. Combine sugar, shortening, butter, reserved melted chocolate, egg yolk and vanilla; beat until well blended. Stir in flour and salt. Roll dough into 1-inch balls. With fork, slightly beat egg white. Dip each ball into egg white; roll in nuts to coat. Place about 1-inch apart on ungreased cookie sheet. Press center of each cookie with thumb to make indentation.

3. Bake 10 to 12 minutes or until set. Remove from oven; immediately place several chocolate chips in center of each cookie. Carefully remove from cookie sheet to wire rack. After several minutes, swirl melted chocolate in each thumbprint. Cool completely.
Makes about 2½ dozen cookies

Crispy Oat Drops

1 cup (2 sticks) butter or margarine, softened
½ cup granulated sugar
½ cup firmly packed light brown sugar
1 large egg
2 cups all-purpose flour
½ cup quick-cooking or old-fashioned oats,
   uncooked
1 teaspoon cream of tartar
½ teaspoon baking soda
¼ teaspoon salt
1¾ cups "M&M's"® Semi-Sweet Chocolate Mini
   Baking Bits
1 cup toasted rice cereal
½ cup shredded coconut
½ cup coarsely chopped pecans

Preheat oven to 350°F. In large bowl cream butter and sugars until light and fluffy; beat in egg. In medium bowl combine flour, oats, cream of tartar, baking soda and salt; blend flour mixture into creamed mixture. Stir in "M&M's"® Semi-Sweet Chocolate Mini Baking Bits, cereal, coconut and pecans. Drop by heaping tablespoonfuls about 2 inches apart onto ungreased cookie sheets. Bake 10 to 13 minutes or until lightly browned. Cool completely on wire racks. Store in tightly covered container. *Makes about 4 dozen cookies*

Mocha Crinkles

1⅓ cups firmly packed light brown sugar
½ cup vegetable oil
¼ cup low-fat sour cream
1 egg
1 teaspoon vanilla
1¾ cups all-purpose flour
¾ cup unsweetened cocoa powder
2 teaspoons instant espresso or coffee granules
1 teaspoon baking soda
¼ teaspoon salt
⅛ teaspoon ground black pepper
½ cup powdered sugar

1. Beat brown sugar and oil in medium bowl with electric mixer. Mix in sour cream, egg and vanilla. Set aside.

2. Mix flour, cocoa, espresso, baking soda, salt and pepper in another medium bowl.

3. Add flour mixture to brown sugar mixture; mix well. Refrigerate dough until firm, 3 to 4 hours.

4. Preheat oven to 350°F. Place powdered sugar in shallow bowl. Set aside. Cut dough into 1-inch pieces; roll into balls. Roll balls in powdered sugar.

5. Bake on ungreased cookie sheets 10 to 12 minutes or until tops of cookies are firm to touch. *Do not overbake.* Cool on wire racks.

Makes 6 dozen cookies

Peanut Gems

2½ cups all-purpose flour
1 teaspoon baking powder
⅛ teaspoon salt
1 cup butter, softened
1 cup packed light brown sugar
2 eggs
2 teaspoons vanilla
1½ cups cocktail peanuts, finely chopped
Powdered sugar (optional)

Preheat oven to 350°F. Combine flour, baking powder and salt in small bowl.

Beat butter in large bowl with electric mixer at medium speed until smooth. Gradually beat in brown sugar; increase speed to medium-high and beat until light and fluffy. Beat in eggs, 1 at a time, until fluffy. Beat in vanilla. Gradually stir in flour mixture until blended. Stir in peanuts until blended.

Drop heaping tablespoonfuls of dough about 1 inch apart onto ungreased cookie sheets; flatten slightly with hands.

Bake 12 minutes or until set. Let cookies stand on cookie sheets 5 minutes; transfer to wire racks to cool completely. Dust cookies with powdered sugar, if desired. Store in airtight container.

Makes about 2½ dozen cookies

Mocha Crinkles

Almond Milk Chocolate Chippers

½ cup slivered almonds
1¼ cups all-purpose flour
½ teaspoon baking soda
½ teaspoon salt
½ cup butter, softened
½ cup firmly packed light brown sugar
⅓ cup granulated sugar
1 egg
2 tablespoons almond-flavored liqueur
1 cup milk chocolate chips

1. Preheat oven to 350°F. To toast almonds, spread on baking sheet. Bake 8 to 10 minutes or until golden brown, stirring frequently. Remove almonds from pan and cool; set aside.

2. *Increase oven temperature to 375°F.* Place flour, baking soda and salt in small bowl; stir to combine.

3. Beat butter, brown sugar and granulated sugar in large bowl with electric mixer at medium speed until light and fluffy. Beat in egg until well blended. Beat in liqueur. Gradually add flour mixture. Beat at low speed until well blended. Stir in chips and almonds with spoon.

4. Drop rounded teaspoonfuls of dough 2 inches apart onto ungreased cookie sheets.

5. Bake 9 to 10 minutes or until edges are golden brown. Let cookies stand on cookie sheets 2 minutes. Remove cookies with spatula to wire racks; cool completely.   *Makes about 3 dozen cookies*

Frosty's Colorful Cookies

1¼ cups firmly packed light brown sugar
¾ Butter Flavor* CRISCO® Stick or ¾ cup
    Butter Flavor CRISCO® all-vegetable
    shortening
2 tablespoons milk
1 tablespoon vanilla
1 egg
1¾ cups all-purpose flour
1 teaspoon salt
¾ teaspoon baking soda
2 cups red and green candy-coated chocolate
    pieces

*Butter Flavor Crisco® is artificially flavored.

1. Heat oven to 375°F. Place sheets of foil on countertop for cooling cookies.

2. Place brown sugar, ¾ cup shortening, milk and vanilla in large bowl. Beat at medium speed of electric mixer until well blended. Add egg; beat well.

3. Combine flour, salt and baking soda. Add to shortening mixture; beat at low speed just until blended. Stir in candy-coated chocolate pieces.

4. Drop dough by rounded measuring tablespoonfuls 3 inches apart onto ungreased baking sheets.

5. Bake one baking sheet at a time at 375°F for 8 to 10 minutes for chewy cookies, or 11 to 13 minutes for crisp cookies. *Do not overbake.* Cool 2 minutes on baking sheet. Remove cookies to foil to cool completely.   *Makes about 3 dozen cookies*

Almond Milk Chocolate Chippers

Cookie Jar Classics

Cookie Jar Classics

Two-Toned Spritz Cookies

1 square (1 ounce) unsweetened chocolate, coarsely chopped
1 cup (2 sticks) butter, softened
1 cup sugar
1 egg
1 teaspoon vanilla
2¼ cups all-purpose flour
¼ teaspoon salt

Melt chocolate in small heavy saucepan over low heat, stirring constantly; set aside. Beat butter and sugar in large bowl until light and fluffy. Beat in egg and vanilla. Combine flour and salt in medium bowl; gradually add to butter mixture. Reserve 2 cups dough. Beat chocolate into dough in bowl until smooth. Cover both doughs and refrigerate until firm enough to handle, about 20 minutes.

Preheat oven to 400°F. Roll out vanilla dough between two sheets of waxed paper to ½-inch thickness. Cut into 5×4-inch rectangles. Place chocolate dough on sheet of waxed paper. Using waxed paper to hold dough, roll back and forth to form a log about 1 inch in diameter. Cut into 5-inch-long logs. Place chocolate log in center of vanilla rectangle. Wrap vanilla dough around log and fit into cookie press fitted with star disc. Press dough onto ungreased cookie sheets 1½ inches apart. Bake about 10 minutes or until just set. Remove cookies with spatula to wire racks; cool completely.

Makes about 4 dozen cookies

Molasses Spice Cookies

1 cup granulated sugar
¾ cup shortening
¼ cup molasses
1 egg, beaten
2 cups all-purpose flour
2 teaspoons baking soda
1 teaspoon ground cinnamon
1 teaspoon ground cloves
1 teaspoon ground ginger
¼ teaspoon dry mustard
¼ teaspoon salt
½ cup granulated brown sugar

1. Preheat oven to 375°F. Grease cookie sheets; set aside.

2. Beat granulated sugar and shortening about 5 minutes in large bowl until light and fluffy. Add molasses and egg; beat until fluffy.

3. Combine flour, baking soda, cinnamon, cloves, ginger, mustard and salt in medium bowl. Add to shortening mixture; mix until just combined.

4. Place brown sugar in shallow dish. Roll tablespoonfuls of dough into 1-inch balls; roll in sugar to coat. Place 2 inches apart on prepared cookie sheets. Bake 15 minutes or until lightly browned. Let cookies stand on cookie sheets 2 minutes. Remove cookies to wire racks; cool completely.

Makes about 6 dozen cookies

Two-Toned Spritz Cookies

Hershey's Great American Chocolate Chip Cookies

1 cup (2 sticks) butter, softened
¾ cup granulated sugar
¾ cup packed light brown sugar
1 teaspoon vanilla extract
2 eggs
2¼ cups all-purpose flour
1 teaspoon baking soda
½ teaspoon salt
2 cups (12-ounce package) HERSHEY'S Semi-Sweet Chocolate Chips
1 cup chopped nuts (optional)

Heat oven to 375°F. Beat butter, granulated sugar, brown sugar and vanilla in large bowl until creamy. Add eggs; beat well. Stir together flour, baking soda and salt; gradually add to butter mixture, beating well. Stir in chocolate chips and nuts, if desired. Drop dough by rounded teaspoonfuls onto ungreased cookie sheet. Bake 8 to 10 minutes or until lightly browned. Cool slightly; remove from cookie sheet to wire rack. Cool completely.

Makes about 6 dozen cookies

Maple Walnut Meringues

⅓ cup powdered sugar
½ cup plus ⅓ cup ground walnuts, divided
¾ cup packed light brown sugar
3 egg whites, at room temperature
Pinch salt
⅛ teaspoon cream of tartar
1 teaspoon maple extract

Place 1 oven rack in the top third of oven and 1 oven rack in the bottom third of oven. Preheat oven to 300°F. Line 2 large cookie sheets with foil, shiny side up. Stir powdered sugar and ½ cup walnuts with fork in medium bowl; set aside. Crumble brown sugar into small bowl; set aside. Beat egg whites and salt in large bowl with electric mixer at high speed until foamy. Add cream of tartar; beat 30 seconds or until mixture forms soft peaks. Sprinkle brown sugar 1 tablespoon at a time over egg white mixture; beat at high speed until each addition is completely absorbed. Beat 2 to 3 minutes or until mixture forms stiff peaks. Beat in maple extract at low speed. Fold in walnut mixture with large rubber spatula. Drop level tablespoonfuls of dough to form mounds about 1 inch apart on prepared cookie sheets. Sprinkle cookies with remaining ⅓ cup ground walnuts. Bake 25 minutes or until cookies feel dry on surface but remain soft inside. (Rotate cookie sheets from top to bottom halfway through baking time.) Slide foil with cookies onto wire racks; cool completely. Carefully remove cookies from foil. Store in airtight container with wax paper between layers of cookies. Cookies are best the day they are baked.

Makes about 3 dozen cookies

Chocolate Bonanza

Festive Fudge Blossoms

1 box (18.25 ounces) chocolate fudge cake mix
¼ cup butter or margarine, softened
1 egg, slightly beaten
¾ to 1 cup finely chopped walnuts
48 chocolate star candies

Preheat oven to 350°F. Cut butter into cake mix in large bowl until coarse crumbs form. Stir in egg and 2 tablespoons water until well blended. Shape dough into ½-inch balls; roll in walnuts, pressing nuts gently into dough. Place about 2 inches apart onto ungreased baking sheets. Bake cookies 12 minutes or until puffed and nearly set. Place chocolate star in center of each cookie; bake 1 minute. Cool 2 minutes on baking sheet. Remove cookies from baking sheets to wire rack to cool completely.

Makes 4 dozen cookies

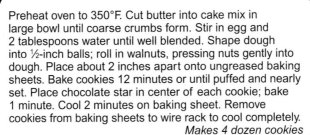

Czech Bear Paws

4 cups toasted ground hazelnuts
2 cups all-purpose flour
1 tablespoon unsweetened cocoa powder
1 teaspoon ground cinnamon
½ teaspoon ground nutmeg
¼ teaspoon salt
1 cup plus 3 teaspoons butter, softened and divided
1 cup powdered sugar
1 egg yolk
½ cup melted chocolate chips
Slivered almonds, halved

1. Preheat oven to 350°F. Place first 6 ingredients in medium bowl; stir.

2. Beat 1 cup butter, sugar and egg yolk in large bowl until light and fluffy. Gradually add flour mixture. Beat until soft dough forms.

3. Grease 3 madeleine pans with remaining softened butter, 1 teaspoon per pan; dust with flour. (If using only 1 madeleine pan, wash, dry, regrease and flour after baking each batch. Cover remaining dough with plastic wrap; let stand at room temperature.) Press level tablespoonfuls of dough into each mold.

4. Bake 12 minutes or until lightly browned. Let cookies stand in pan 3 minutes. Carefully loosen cookies from pan with point of small knife. Invert pan over wire racks; tap lightly to release cookies. Let stand 2 minutes. Turn cookies shell-side up; cool.

5. Pipe squiggle of chocolate on curved end of each cookie; place almonds in chocolate for claws. Let stand 1 hour or until set. Store tightly covered at room temperature.
Makes about 5 dozen cookies

Note: These cookies do not freeze well.

Triple Chocolate Cookies

1 package DUNCAN HINES® Moist Deluxe® Swiss Chocolate Cake Mix
½ cup butter or margarine, melted
1 egg
½ cup semi-sweet chocolate chips
½ cup milk chocolate chips
½ cup coarsely chopped white chocolate
½ cup chopped pecans

1. Preheat oven to 375°F.

2. Combine cake mix, melted butter and egg in large bowl. Beat at low speed with electric mixer until blended. Stir in all 3 chocolates and pecans.

3. Drop by rounded tablespoonfuls onto ungreased baking sheets. Bake at 375°F 9 to 11 minutes. Cool 1 minute on baking sheet. Remove to cooling racks.
Makes 3½ to 4 dozen cookies

Tip: Cookies may be stored in an airtight container in freezer for up to 6 months.

Czech Bear Paws

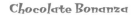

S'more Snack Treats

**44 squares HONEY MAID® Honey Grahams
(2 sleeves)**
**3 tablespoons FLEISCHMANN'S® Original
Margarine**
1 (10-ounce) package marshmallows
¾ cup miniature semisweet chocolate chips

1. Break grahams into bite-size pieces; set aside.

2. Heat margarine in large saucepan over medium heat until melted. Add marshmallows, stirring constantly until melted.

3. Stir broken crackers into marshmallow mixture to coat evenly. Spread mixture into lightly greased 13×9×2-inch pan; sprinkle with chocolate chips, pressing lightly with greased hands.

4. Chill at least 20 minutes before cutting into squares. *Makes 12 s'mores*

Preparation Time: 15 minutes

Cook Time: 20 minutes

Chill Time: 20 minutes

Total Time: 55 minutes

Festive Chocolate Chip Cookies

**1 package DUNCAN HINES® Moist Deluxe®
White Cake Mix**
¼ cup firmly packed light brown sugar
1 egg
¾ cup vegetable oil
**1 package (6 ounces) semi-sweet chocolate
chips**
**½ cup chopped pecans or walnuts
Assorted decors**

1. Preheat oven to 350°F.

2. Combine cake mix, brown sugar, egg and oil in large bowl. Beat at low speed with electric mixer until blended. Stir in chocolate chips and pecans. Form dough into 1½-inch ball. Dip top of ball in decors. Place ball decor-side up on ungreased baking sheets. Repeat with remaining dough placing balls 2 inches apart on baking sheets. Bake at 350°F 10 to 12 minutes or until light golden brown around edges. Cool 2 minutes on baking sheets. Remove to cooling racks. Cool completely. Store in airtight container. *Makes 3 to 3½ dozen cookies*

Tip: Cool baking sheet completely before baking each batch of cookies.

Marshmallow Sandwich Cookies

⅔ cup butter
1¼ cups sugar
¼ cup light corn syrup
1 egg
1 teaspoon vanilla
2 cups all-purpose flour
½ cup unsweetened cocoa powder
2 teaspoons baking soda
¼ teaspoon salt
Sugar for rolling
24 large marshmallows

Preheat oven to 350°F. Beat butter and 1¼ cups sugar in large bowl until light and fluffy. Beat in corn syrup, egg and vanilla. Combine flour, cocoa, baking soda and salt in medium bowl; add to butter mixture. Beat until well blended. Cover and refrigerate dough 15 minutes or until firm enough to roll into balls.

Place sugar in shallow dish. Roll tablespoonfuls of dough into 1-inch balls; roll in sugar to coat. Place cookies 3 inches apart on ungreased cookie sheets. Bake 10 to 12 minutes or until set. Remove cookies to wire rack; cool completely.

To assemble sandwiches, place one marshmallow on flat side of one cookie on paper plate. Microwave at HIGH 12 seconds or until marshmallow just begins to melt. Immediately place another cookie, flat side down, on top of hot marshmallow; press together slightly.

Makes about 2 dozen sandwich cookies

Santa's Chocolate Cookies

1 cup margarine or butter
⅔ cup semisweet chocolate chips
¾ cup sugar
1 egg
½ teaspoon vanilla
2 cups all-purpose flour
Apricot jam, melted semisweet chocolate, chopped almonds, frosting, coconut or colored sprinkles

Preheat oven to 350°F. Melt margarine and chocolate together in small saucepan over low heat or microwave 2 minutes at HIGH until completely melted. Combine chocolate mixture and sugar in large bowl. Add egg and vanilla; stir well. Add flour; stir well. Refrigerate 30 minutes or until firm.

Shape dough into 1-inch balls. Place 1 inch apart on ungreased cookie sheets. If desired, flatten balls with bottom of drinking glass, shape into logs or make a depression in center and fill with apricot jam.

Bake 8 to 10 minutes or until set. Remove to wire racks to cool completely. Decorate as desired with melted chocolate, almonds, frosting, coconut and colored sprinkles. *Makes about 3 dozen cookies*

Nutty Clusters

2 squares (1 ounce *each*) unsweetened chocolate
½ cup butter, softened
1 cup sugar
1 egg
⅓ cup buttermilk
1 teaspoon vanilla
1¾ cups all-purpose flour
½ teaspoon baking soda
1 cup mixed salted nuts, chopped
Easy Chocolate Icing (recipe follows)

Preheat oven to 400°F. Line cookie sheets with parchment paper or leave ungreased. Melt chocolate in top of double boiler over hot, not boiling, water. Remove from heat; cool. Beat butter and sugar in large bowl until smooth. Beat in egg, chocolate, buttermilk and vanilla until light. Stir in flour, baking soda and nuts. Drop dough by teaspoonfuls 2 inches apart onto cookie sheets. Bake 8 to 10 minutes or until almost no imprint remains when touched. Immediately remove cookies from cookie sheets to wire racks. While cookies bake, prepare Easy Chocolate Icing. Frost cookies while still warm.

Makes about 4 dozen cookies

Easy Chocolate Icing

2 squares (1 ounce *each*) unsweetened chocolate
2 tablespoons butter or margarine
2 cups powdered sugar
2 to 3 tablespoons water

Melt chocolate and butter in small heavy saucepan over low heat, stirring until completely melted. Add powdered sugar and water, mixing until smooth.

Chocolate Macaroons

1 can (8 ounces) almond paste
½ cup powdered sugar
2 egg whites
12 ounces semisweet baking chocolate or chips, melted
2 tablespoons all-purpose flour
Powdered sugar (optional)

Preheat oven to 300°F. Line cookie sheets with parchment paper; set aside.

Beat almond paste, sugar and egg whites in large bowl with electric mixer at medium speed 1 minute. Beat in chocolate until well combined. Beat in flour at low speed.

Spoon dough into pastry bag fitted with rosette tip. Pipe 1½-inch spirals 1 inch apart onto prepared cookie sheets. Pipe all cookies at once; dough will get stiff upon standing.

Bake 20 minutes or until set. Carefully remove parchment paper to countertop; cool completely.

Peel cookies off parchment paper. Sprinkle powdered sugar over cookies, if desired.

Makes about 3 dozen cookies

Candy Cane Cookies

1 cup sugar
⅔ cup FLEISCHMANN'S® Original Margarine, softened
½ cup EGG BEATERS® Healthy Real Egg Substitute
2 teaspoons vanilla extract
1 teaspoon almond extract
3 cups all-purpose flour
1 teaspoon DAVIS® Baking Powder
½ teaspoon red food coloring

1. Beat sugar and margarine in large bowl with mixer at medium speed until creamy. Beat in egg substitute, vanilla and almond extracts. Mix flour and baking powder; stir into margarine mixture.

continued on page 44

2. Divide dough in half; tint half with red food coloring. Wrap each half and refrigerate at least 2 hours.

3. Divide each half into 32 pieces. Roll each piece into a 5-inch rope. Twist 1 red and 1 white rope together and bend 1 end to form candy cane shape. Place on ungreased baking sheets.

4. Bake in preheated 350°F oven for 8 to 10 minutes or just until set and lightly golden. Remove from sheets; cool on wire racks. Store in airtight container.

Makes 32 cookies

Helpful Hint

Looking for something different to take to all your holiday gatherings? Decorate a metal tin with rubber stamps for a crafty look and fill it with candy cane cookies and an assortment of flavored coffees. Perfect for a "homey" hostess gift.

Cocoa Kiss Cookies

  1 cup (2 sticks) butter or margarine, softened
  ⅔ cup sugar
  1 teaspoon vanilla extract
 1⅔ cups all-purpose flour
  ¼ cup HERSHEY₃S Cocoa
  1 cup finely chopped pecans
  1 bag (9 ounces) HERSHEY₃S KISSES® Milk Chocolates
  Powdered sugar

1. Beat butter, sugar and vanilla in large bowl until creamy. Stir together flour and cocoa; gradually add to butter mixture, beating until blended. Add pecans; beat until well blended. Refrigerate dough about 1 hour or until firm enough to handle.

2. Heat oven to 375°F. Remove wrappers from chocolate pieces. Mold scant tablespoon of dough around each chocolate piece, covering completely. Shape into balls. Place on ungreased cookie sheet.

3. Bake 10 to 12 minutes or until set. Cool slightly, about 1 minute; remove from cookie sheet to wire rack. Cool completely. Roll in powdered sugar. Roll in sugar again just before serving, if desired.

Makes about 4½ dozen cookies

Top to bottom: Cocoa Kiss Cookies and Hershey₃s Great American Chocolate Chip Cookies (page 30)

Slice 'n' Bake Ginger Wafers

½ **cup butter or margarine, softened**
1 **cup packed brown sugar**
¼ **cup light molasses**
1 **egg**
2 **teaspoons ground ginger**
1 **teaspoon grated orange peel**
¼ **teaspoon salt**
¼ **teaspoon ground cinnamon**
¼ **teaspoon ground cloves**
2 **cups all-purpose flour**

1. Beat butter, sugar and molasses in large bowl until light and fluffy. Add egg, ginger, orange peel, salt, cinnamon and cloves; beat until well blended. Stir in flour until well blended. (Dough will be very stiff.)

2. Divide dough in half. Roll each half into 8×1½-inch log. Wrap logs in waxed paper or plastic wrap; refrigerate at least 5 hours or up to 3 days.

3. Preheat oven to 350°F. Cut dough into ¼-inch-thick slices. Place about 2 inches apart on ungreased baking sheets. Bake 12 to 14 minutes or until set. Remove from baking sheet to wire rack to cool.
Makes about 4½ dozen cookies

Serving Suggestion: Dip half of each cookie in melted white chocolate or drizzle cookies with a glaze of 1¼ cups powdered sugar and 2 tablespoons orange juice. Or, cut cookie dough into ⅛-inch-thick slices; bake and sandwich melted caramel candy or peanut butter between cookies.

Snowball Cookies

1 **cup margarine or butter, softened**
1 **cup sugar**
1 **teaspoon vanilla extract**
2 **cups all-purpose flour**
1½ **cups PLANTERS® Pecans, finely ground**
¼ **teaspoon salt**
½ **cup powdered sugar**

1. Beat margarine, sugar and vanilla in large bowl with mixer at medium speed until creamy. Blend in flour, pecans and salt. Refrigerate 1 hour.

2. Shape dough into 1-inch balls. Place on ungreased baking sheets, 2 inches apart. Bake in preheated 350°F oven for 10 to 12 minutes. Remove from sheets; cool on wire racks. Dust with powdered sugar. Store in airtight container.
Makes 6 dozen cookies

Preparation Time: 15 minutes

Chill Time: 1 hour

Cook Time: 10 minutes

Total Time: 1 hour and 25 minutes

Slice 'n' Bake Ginger Wafers

Rum Fruitcake Cookies

1 cup sugar
¾ cup vegetable shortening
3 eggs
⅓ cup orange juice
1 tablespoon rum extract
3 cups all-purpose flour
2 teaspoons baking powder
1 teaspoon baking soda
1 teaspoon salt
2 cups (8 ounces) candied fruit
1 cup raisins
1 cup nuts, coarsely chopped

1. Preheat oven to 375°F. Lightly grease cookie sheets; set aside. Beat sugar and shortening in large bowl until fluffy. Add eggs, orange juice and rum extract; beat 2 minutes longer.

2. Combine flour, baking powder, baking soda and salt in small bowl. Add fruit, raisins and nuts. Stir into creamed mixture. Drop dough by rounded teaspoonfuls 2 inches apart onto prepared cookie sheets. Bake 10 to 12 minutes or until golden. Let cookies stand on cookie sheets 2 minutes. Remove to wire rack; cool completely.

Makes about 6 dozen cookies

Holiday Wreath Cookies

1 package (20 ounces) refrigerated sugar
   cookie dough
2 cups shredded coconut
2 to 3 drops green food color
1 container (16 ounces) ready-to-spread
   French vanilla frosting
Green sugar or small cinnamon candies

1. Preheat oven to 350°F. Divide cookie dough in half (keep half of dough refrigerated until needed). Roll dough out on well-floured surface to ⅛-inch-thick rectangle. Cut with cookie cutters to resemble wreaths. Repeat with remaining half of dough.

2. Place cookies about 2 inches apart on ungreased baking sheets. Bake 7 to 9 minutes or until edges are lightly browned. Remove cookies from baking sheets to wire rack to cool completely.

3. Place coconut in resealable plastic food storage bag. Add food color; seal bag and shake until coconut is evenly colored. Frost cookies with frosting and decorate with coconut or green sugar and cinnamon candies.

Makes about 2 dozen cookies

Prep and Bake Time: 30 minutes

Rum Fruitcake Cookies

Fruitcake Slices

1 cup butter or margarine, softened
1 cup powdered sugar
1 egg
1 teaspoon vanilla extract
1½ cups coarsely chopped candied fruit
(fruitcake mix)
½ cup coarsely chopped walnuts
2½ cups all-purpose unsifted flour, divided
¾ to 1 cup flaked coconut

Beat butter in large bowl with electric mixer at medium speed until smooth. Add powdered sugar; beat until well blended. Add egg and vanilla; beat until well blended.

Combine candied fruit and walnuts in medium bowl. Stir ¼ cup flour into fruit mixture. Add remaining 2¼ cups flour to butter mixture; beat at low speed until blended. Stir in fruit mixture with spoon.

Shape dough into 2 logs, each about 2 inches in diameter and 5½ inches long. Spread coconut evenly on sheet of waxed paper. Roll logs in coconut, coating evenly. Wrap each log in plastic wrap. Refrigerate 2 to 3 hours or overnight, or freeze up to 1 month. (Let frozen logs stand at room temperature about 10 minutes before slicing and baking.)

Preheat oven to 350°F. Grease cookie sheets. Cut logs into ¼-inch-thick slices; place 1 inch apart on cookie sheets.

Bake 13 to 15 minutes or until edges are golden brown. Transfer to wire racks to cool.

Makes about 4 dozen cookies

Honey Ginger Snaps

2 cups all-purpose flour
1 tablespoon ground ginger
2 teaspoons baking soda
⅛ teaspoon salt
⅛ teaspoon ground cloves
½ cup vegetable shortening
¼ cup butter, softened
1½ cups sugar, divided
¼ cup honey
1 egg
1 teaspoon vanilla

Preheat oven to 350°F. Grease cookie sheets. Combine flour, ginger, baking soda, salt and cloves in medium bowl.

Beat shortening and butter in large bowl with electric mixer at medium speed until smooth. Gradually beat in 1 cup sugar until blended; increase speed to high and beat until light and fluffy. Beat in honey, egg and vanilla until fluffy. Gradually stir in flour mixture until blended.

Shape mixture into 1-inch balls. Place remaining ½ cup sugar in shallow bowl; roll balls in sugar to coat. Place 2 inches apart on prepared cookie sheets.

Bake 10 minutes or until golden brown. Let cookies stand on cookie sheets 5 minutes; transfer to wire racks to cool completely.

Makes 42 cookies

Fruitcake Slices

Oatmeal Almond Balls

⅓ cup honey
2 egg whites
½ teaspoon ground cinnamon
⅛ teaspoon salt
1½ cups uncooked quick oats
¼ cup sliced almonds, toasted

1. Preheat oven to 350°F. Combine honey, egg whites, cinnamon and salt in large bowl; mix well. Add oats and toasted almonds; mix well.

2. Drop by rounded teaspoonfuls onto ungreased nonstick cooking sheet. Bake 12 minutes or until lightly browned. Remove to wire rack to cool.

Makes 24 servings

Thumbprint Cookies

1 cup butter or margarine
¼ cup sugar
1 teaspoon almond extract
2 cups all-purpose flour
½ teaspoon salt
1 cup finely chopped nuts, if desired
SMUCKER'S® Preserves or Jams (any flavor)

Combine butter and sugar; beat until light and fluffy. Blend in almond extract. Add flour and salt; mix well.

Shape level tablespoonfuls of dough into balls; roll in nuts. Place on ungreased cookie sheets; flatten slightly. Indent centers; fill with preserves or jams.

Bake at 400°F for 10 to 12 minutes or just until lightly browned. *Makes 2½ dozen cookies*

Snow-Covered Almond Crescents

1 cup (2 sticks) margarine or butter, softened
¾ cup powdered sugar
½ teaspoon almond extract *or* 2 teaspoons vanilla extract
2 cups all-purpose flour
¼ teaspoon salt (optional)
1 cup QUAKER® Oats (quick or old-fashioned, uncooked)
½ cup finely chopped almonds
Additional powdered sugar

Preheat oven to 325°F. Beat margarine, ¾ cup powdered sugar and almond extract until fluffy. Add flour and salt; mix until well blended. Stir in oats and almonds. Shape level measuring tablespoonfuls of dough into crescents. Place on ungreased cookie sheet about 2 inches apart.

Bake 14 to 17 minutes or until bottoms are light golden brown. Remove to wire rack. Sift additional powdered sugar generously over warm cookies. Cool completely. Store tightly covered.

Makes about 4 dozen cookies

Oatmeal Almond Balls

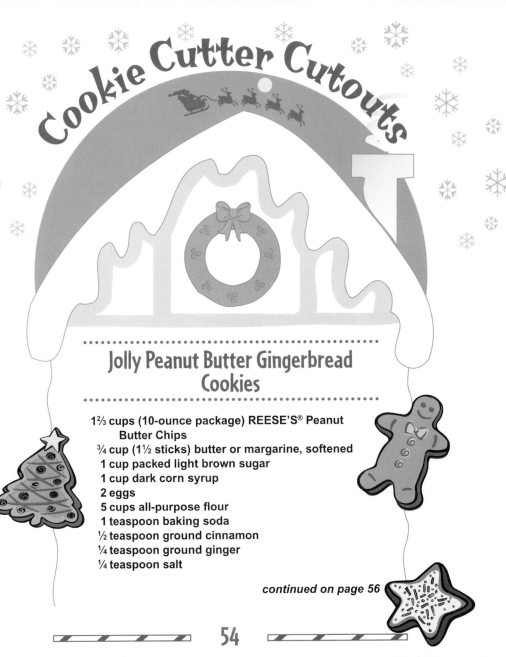

Cookie Cutter Cutouts

Jolly Peanut Butter Gingerbread Cookies

1⅔ cups (10-ounce package) REESE'S® Peanut
    Butter Chips
¾ cup (1½ sticks) butter or margarine, softened
1 cup packed light brown sugar
1 cup dark corn syrup
2 eggs
5 cups all-purpose flour
1 teaspoon baking soda
½ teaspoon ground cinnamon
¼ teaspoon ground ginger
¼ teaspoon salt

continued on page 56

Jolly Peanut Butter Gingerbread Cookies, continued

1. Place peanut butter chips in small microwave-safe bowl. Microwave at HIGH (100%) 1 to 2 minutes or until chips are melted when stirred. Beat melted peanut butter chips and butter in large bowl until well blended. Add brown sugar, corn syrup and eggs; beat until light and fluffy. Stir together flour, baking soda, cinnamon, ginger and salt. Add half of flour mixture to butter mixture; beat on low speed of electric mixer until smooth. Stir in remaining flour mixture with wooden spoon until well blended. Divide into thirds; wrap each in plastic wrap. Refrigerate at least 1 hour or until dough is firm enough to roll.

2. Heat oven to 325°F.

3. Roll 1 dough portion at a time to ⅛-inch thickness on lightly floured surface. Cut into holiday shapes with floured cookie cutters. Place on ungreased cookie sheet.

4. Bake 10 to 12 minutes or until set and lightly browned. Cool slightly; remove from cookie sheet to wire rack. Cool completely. Frost and decorate as desired. *Makes about 6 dozen cookies*

Holiday Bits Cutout Cookies

1 cup (2 sticks) butter or margarine, softened
1 cup sugar
2 eggs
2 teaspoons vanilla extract
2½ cups all-purpose flour
½ teaspoon baking powder
½ teaspoon salt
HERSHEY₃S Holiday Candy Coated Bits

1. Beat butter, sugar, eggs and vanilla in large bowl on low speed of electric mixer just until blended. Stir together flour, baking powder and salt; add to butter mixture, stirring until well blended.

2. Divide dough in half. Cover; refrigerate 1 to 2 hours or until firm enough to handle. Heat oven to 400°F. On lightly floured surface, roll each half of the dough to about ¼ inch thick.

3. Cut into tree, wreath, star or other shapes with 2½-inch cookie cutters. Place on ungreased cookie sheet. Press candy coated bits into cutouts.

4. Bake 6 to 8 minutes or until edges are firm and bottoms are very lightly browned. Remove from cookie sheet to wire rack. Cool completely. *Makes about 3½ dozen cookies*

Holiday Bits Cutout Cookies

Christmas Cookie Pops

1 package (20 ounces) refrigerated sugar
   cookie dough
All-purpose flour (optional)
20 to 24 (4-inch) lollipop sticks
Royal Icing (recipe follows)
6 ounces almond bark (vanilla or chocolate),
   or butterscotch chips
Vegetable shortening
Assorted small candies

1. Preheat oven to 350°F. Grease cookie sheets; set aside.

2. Remove dough from wrapper according to package directions.

3. Sprinkle dough with flour to minimize sticking, if necessary. Cut dough in half. Reserve 1 half; refrigerate remaining dough.

4. Roll reserved dough to ⅓-inch thickness. Cut out cookies using 3¼- or 3½-inch Christmas cookie cutters. Place lollipop sticks on cookies so that tips of sticks are imbedded in cookies. Carefully turn cookies with spatula so sticks are in back; place on prepared cookie sheets. Repeat with remaining dough.

5. Bake 7 to 11 minutes or until edges are lightly browned. Cool cookies on sheets 2 minutes. Remove cookies to wire racks; cool completely.

6. Prepare Royal Icing.

7. Melt almond bark in medium microwavable bowl according to package directions. Add 1 or more tablespoons shortening if coating is too thick. Hold cookies over bowl; spoon coating over cookies. Scrape excess coating from cookie edges. Decorate with Royal Icing and small candies immediately. Place cookies on wire racks set over waxed paper; let dry. *Makes 20 to 24 cookies*

Royal Icing

2 to 3 egg whites*
2 to 4 cups powdered sugar
1 tablespoon lemon juice
Liquid food coloring (optional)

* Use only grade A clean, uncracked eggs.

Beat 2 egg whites in medium bowl with electric mixer until peaks just begin to hold their shape. Add 2 cups sugar and lemon juice; beat for 1 minute. If consistency is too thin for piping, gradually add more sugar until desired result is achieved; if it is too thick, add another egg white. Divide icing among several small bowls and tint to desired colors. Keep bowls tightly covered until ready to use.

Cookie Cutter Cutouts

Cookie Cutter Cutouts

Christmas Tree Platter

Christmas Ornament Cookie Dough
(recipe follows)
2 cups sifted powdered sugar
2 tablespoons milk or lemon juice
Assorted food colors, colored sugars and
assorted small decors

2¼ **cups all-purpose flour**
¼ **teaspoon salt**
1 **cup granulated sugar**
¾ **cup butter or margarine, softened**
1 **egg**
1 **teaspoon vanilla**
1 **teaspoon almond extract**

1. Prepare Christmas Ornament Cookie Dough. Divide dough in half. Reserve 1 half; refrigerate remaining dough. Roll reserved half of dough to ⅛-inch thickness.

2. Preheat oven to 350°F. Cut out tree shapes with cookie cutters. Place on ungreased cookie sheets.

3. Bake 10 to 12 minutes or until edges are lightly browned. Remove to wire racks; cool completely.

4. Repeat with remaining half of dough. Reroll scraps; cut into small circles for ornaments, squares and rectangles for gift boxes and tree trunks.

5. Bake 8 to 12 minutes, depending on size of cookies.

6. Mix powdered sugar and milk for icing. Tint most of icing green and a smaller amount red or other colors for ornaments and boxes. Spread green icing on trees. Sprinkle ornaments and boxes with colored sugars or decorate as desired.

7. Arrange cookies on flat platter to resemble tree as shown in photo.

Makes about 1 dozen cookies

Combine flour and salt in medium bowl. Beat sugar and butter in large bowl at medium speed of electric mixer until fluffy. Beat in egg, vanilla and almond extract. Gradually add flour mixture. Beat at low speed until well blended. Form dough into 2 discs; wrap in plastic wrap and refrigerate 30 minutes or until firm.

Helpful Hint

Use these beautiful Christmas Tree Platter cookies as your centerpiece for this holiday's family dinner. They're sure to receive lots of "oohs" and "ahs!"

Stained Glass Cookies

½ cup FLEISCHMANN'S® Original Margarine, softened
½ cup sugar
½ cup honey
¼ cup EGG BEATERS® Healthy Real Egg Substitute
1 teaspoon vanilla extract
3 cups all-purpose flour
1 teaspoon DAVIS® Baking Powder
½ teaspoon baking soda
½ teaspoon salt
5 (.90-ounce) rolls Five Flavor or Fancy Fruits LIFE SAVERS® Candy

1. Beat together margarine, sugar, honey, egg substitute and vanilla in bowl with mixer until creamy. Mix in flour, baking powder, baking soda and salt. Cover; refrigerate at least 2 hours.

2. Roll dough on a lightly floured surface to ¼-inch thickness. Cut dough into desired shapes with 2½- to 3-inch floured cookie cutters. Trace a smaller version of cookie shape on dough leaving a ½- to ¾-inch border of dough. Cut out and remove dough from center of cookies; set aside. Place cut-out shapes on baking sheets lined with foil. Repeat with reserved dough, re-rolling scraps as necessary.

3. Crush each color of candy separately between two layers of wax paper. Spoon crushed candy inside centers of cut-out cookie shapes.

4. Bake in preheated 350°F oven for 6 to 8 minutes or until candy is melted and cookies are lightly browned. Cool cookies completely before removing from foil.   *Makes 3½ dozen*

Preparation Time: 1 hour

Chill Time: 2 hours

Cook Time: 6 minutes

Total Time: 3 hours and 6 minutes

Butter Cookies

¾ cup butter or margarine, softened
¼ cup granulated sugar
¼ cup packed light brown sugar
1 egg yolk
1¾ cups all-purpose flour
¾ teaspoon baking powder
⅛ teaspoon salt

1. Combine butter, sugars and egg yolk in medium bowl. Add flour, baking powder and salt; mix well. Cover; refrigerate until firm, about 4 hours or overnight.

2. Preheat oven to 350°F.

3. Roll dough on lightly floured surface to ¼-inch thickness; cut into desired shapes with cookie cutters. Place on ungreased cookie sheets.

4. Bake 8 to 10 minutes or until edges begin to brown. Remove to wire racks; cool completely.
Makes about 2 dozen cookies

Stained Glass Cookies

Extra-Special Cookies

Molded Scotch Shortbread

1½ **cups all-purpose flour**
¼ **teaspoon salt**
¾ **cup butter, softened**
⅓ **cup sugar**
1 **egg**

Preheat oven to temperature recommended by shortbread mold manufacturer. Combine flour and salt in medium bowl. Beat butter and sugar in large bowl with electric mixer at medium speed until light and fluffy. Beat in egg. Gradually add flour mixture; beat at low speed. Spray 10-inch ceramic shortbread mold with nonstick cooking spray. Press dough firmly into mold. Bake, cool and remove from mold according to manufacturer's directions.

Makes 1 shortbread mold

Danish Cookie Rings

½ cup blanched almonds
2 cups all-purpose flour
¾ cup sugar
¼ teaspoon baking powder
1 cup butter, cut into small pieces
1 egg
1 tablespoon milk
1 tablespoon vanilla
16 candied green cherries, cut into halves
8 candied red cherries, cut into halves

Grease cookie sheets; set aside. Process almonds in food processor until ground, but not pasty. Place almonds, flour, sugar and baking powder in large bowl. Cut butter into flour mixture with pastry blender or 2 knives until mixture is crumbly.

Beat egg, milk and vanilla in small bowl with fork until well blended. Add egg mixture to flour mixture; stir until soft dough forms.

Spoon dough into pastry bag fitted with medium star tip. Pipe 3-inch rings 2 inches apart onto prepared cookie sheets. Refrigerate rings 15 minutes or until firm.

Preheat oven to 375°F. Cut each green cherry half into 4 slivers. Cut each red cherry half into quarters. Press red cherry quarter onto each ring where ends meet. Arrange 2 green cherry slivers on either side of red cherry to form leaves. Bake 8 to 10 minutes or until golden. Remove cookies to wire racks; cool completely. *Makes about 5 dozen cookies*

Mocha Biscotti

2½ cups all-purpose flour
½ cup unsweetened cocoa
2 teaspoons DAVIS® Baking Powder
1¼ cups sugar
¾ cup egg substitute
¼ cup margarine or butter, melted
4 teaspoons instant coffee powder
½ teaspoon vanilla extract
⅓ cup PLANTERS® Slivered Almonds, chopped
Powdered sugar (optional)

1. Mix flour, cocoa and baking powder in small bowl; set aside.

2. Beat sugar, egg substitute, melted margarine, coffee powder and vanilla in large bowl with mixer at medium speed for 2 minutes. Stir in flour mixture and almonds.

3. Divide dough in half. Shape each portion of dough with floured hands into 14×2-inch log on greased baking sheet. (Dough will be sticky). Bake in preheated 350°F oven for 25 minutes.

4. Remove from oven and cut each log on a diagonal into 16 (1-inch) slices. Place biscotti, cut-side up, on baking sheets; return to oven and bake 10 to 15 minutes more on each side or until lightly toasted.

5. Remove from sheets. Cool completely on wire racks. Dust biscotti tops with powdered sugar if desired. Store in airtight container.
Makes 32 biscotti

Danish Cookie Rings

Linzer Sandwich Cookies

1⅓ cups all-purpose flour
¼ teaspoon baking powder
¼ teaspoon salt
¾ cup granulated sugar
½ cup butter, softened
1 egg
1 teaspoon vanilla
    Powdered sugar (optional)
    Seedless raspberry jam

Combine flour, baking powder and salt in small bowl. Beat granulated sugar and butter in medium bowl until light and fluffy. Beat in egg and vanilla. Gradually add flour mixture. Beat until dough forms. Divide dough in half; cover and chill 2 hours or until firm.

Preheat oven to 375°F. Working with 1 portion at a time, roll out dough on lightly floured surface to ³⁄₁₆-inch thickness. Cut dough into desired shapes with floured cookie cutters. Cut out equal numbers of each shape. (If dough becomes too soft, refrigerate several minutes before continuing.) Cut 1-inch centers out of half the cookies of each shape. Reroll scraps and cut out more cookies. Place cookies 1½ to 2 inches apart on ungreased cookie sheets. Bake 7 to 9 minutes or until edges are lightly brown. Let cookies stand on cookie sheets 1 to 2 minutes. Remove cookies to wire racks; cool.

Sprinkle cookies with holes with powdered sugar, if desired. Spread 1 teaspoon jam on flat side of whole cookies, spreading almost to edges. Place cookies with holes, flat side down, over jam to create sandwich.   *Makes about 2 dozen cookies*

Chunky Butter Christmas Cookies

1¼ cups butter, softened
1 cup packed brown sugar
½ cup dairy sour cream
1 egg
2 teaspoons vanilla
1½ cups all-purpose flour
1 teaspoon baking soda
1 teaspoon salt
1½ cups old fashioned or quick oats, uncooked
1 (10-ounce) package white chocolate pieces
1 cup flaked coconut
1 (3½-ounce) jar macadamia nuts, coarsely chopped

Beat butter and sugar in large bowl until light and fluffy. Blend in sour cream, egg and vanilla. Add combined flour, baking soda and salt; mix well. Stir in oats, white chocolate pieces, coconut and nuts. Drop rounded teaspoonfuls of dough, 2 inches apart, onto ungreased cookie sheet. Bake in preheated 375°F oven 10 to 12 minutes or until edges are lightly browned. Cool 1 minute; remove to cooling rack.

Makes 5 dozen cookies

Favorite recipe from **Wisconsin Milk Marketing Board**

Mincemeat Pastries

3½ cups all-purpose flour
¾ cup granulated sugar
½ teaspoon salt
½ cup (1 stick) butter, chilled
8 tablespoons vegetable shortening
1 cup buttermilk
1 cup mincemeat
¼ cup powdered sugar (optional)

1. Combine flour, granulated sugar and salt in large bowl; set aside.

2. Cut butter into 1-inch chunks. Add butter and shortening to flour mixture. Cut in with pastry blender or 2 knives until mixture resembles coarse crumbs. Drizzle buttermilk over top; toss just until mixture comes together into a ball.

3. Turn out dough onto lightly floured work surface; fold in half and flatten to about ½ inch thick. Knead about eight times. Divide dough in half; press each half into ½-inch-thick disk. Wrap in plastic wrap and refrigerate at least 30 minutes.

4. Let dough rest at room temperature 10 minutes. Preheat oven to 350°F. Lightly grease cookie sheets; set aside. Roll one disk of dough into 18×12-inch rectangle on lightly floured work surface. Cut into 24 (3-inch) squares. Place heaping ½ teaspoon mincemeat in center of each square. Fold one corner about ⅔ of the way over the filling; fold opposite corner ⅔ of the way over the filling.

5. Place 2 inches apart on prepared cookie sheets. Repeat with remaining dough.

6. Bake 20 minutes or until lightly browned. Remove cookies to wire rack; cool completely. Sprinkle tops of pastries lightly with powdered sugar, if desired.
Makes 4 dozen cookies

Banana Crescents

½ cup DOLE® Chopped Almonds, toasted
6 tablespoons sugar, divided
½ cup margarine, cut into pieces
1½ cups plus 2 tablespoons all-purpose flour
⅛ teaspoon salt
1 extra-ripe, medium DOLE® Banana, peeled
2 to 3 ounces semisweet chocolate chips

• Pulverize almonds with 2 tablespoons sugar.

• Beat margarine, almonds, remaining 4 tablespoons sugar, flour and salt.

• Purée banana; add to almond mixture and mix until well blended.

• Roll tablespoonfuls of dough into logs, then shape into crescents. Place on ungreased cookie sheet. Bake in 375°F oven 25 minutes or until golden. Cool on wire rack.

• Melt chocolate in microwavable dish at MEDIUM (50% power) 1½ to 2 minutes, stirring once. Dip ends of cookies in chocolate. Refrigerate until chocolate is set.
Makes 2 dozen cookies

Date Pinwheel Cookies

1¼ cups dates, pitted and finely chopped
¾ cup orange juice
½ cup granulated sugar
1 tablespoon butter
3 cups plus 1 tablespoon all-purpose flour, divided
2 teaspoons vanilla, divided
4 ounces cream cheese
¼ cup vegetable shortening
1 cup packed brown sugar
2 eggs
1 teaspoon baking soda
½ teaspoon salt

1. Heat dates, orange juice, granulated sugar, butter and 1 tablespoon flour in medium saucepan over medium heat. Cook, stirring frequently, 10 minutes or until thick; remove from heat. Stir in 1 teaspoon vanilla; set aside to cool.

2. Beat cream cheese, shortening and brown sugar about 3 minutes in large bowl until light and fluffy. Add eggs and remaining 1 teaspoon vanilla; beat 2 minutes longer.

3. Combine 3 cups flour, baking soda and salt in medium bowl. Add to shortening mixture; stir just until blended. Divide dough in half. Roll one half of dough on lightly floured work surface into 12×9-inch rectangle. Spread half of date mixture over dough. Spread evenly, leaving ¼-inch border on top short edge. Starting at short side, tightly roll up dough jelly-roll style. Wrap in plastic wrap; freeze for at least 1 hour. Repeat with remaining dough.

4. Preheat oven to 350°F. Grease cookie sheets. Unwrap dough. Using heavy thread or dental floss, cut dough into ¼-inch slices. Place slices 1 inch apart on prepared cookie sheets.

5. Bake 12 minutes or until lightly browned. Let cookies stand on cookie sheets 2 minutes. Remove cookies to wire rack; cool completely.

Makes 6 dozen cookies

Helpful Hint

Wrap rolls of dough in plastic wrap and twist the ends tightly to seal. Place wrapped rolls in tall plastic drinking glasses before freezing so rolls will not flatten from resting on freezer shelf.

Acknowledgments

The publishers would like to thank the companies and organizations listed below for the use of their recipes and photographs in this publication.

Blue Diamond Growers®

Dole Food Company, Inc.

Duncan Hines® brand is a registered trademark of Aurora Foods Inc.

Hershey Foods Corporation

HONEY MAID® Honey Grahams

Kahlúa® Liqueur

M&M/MARS

PLANTERS® Baking Nuts

The Procter & Gamble Company

The Quaker® Kitchens

The J.M. Smucker Company

Wisconsin Milk Marketing Board

Index

METRIC CONVERSION CHART

VOLUME MEASUREMENTS (dry)

1/8 teaspoon	= 0.5 mL
1/4 teaspoon	= 1 mL
1/2 teaspoon	= 2 mL
3/4 teaspoon	= 4 mL
1 teaspoon	= 5 mL
1 tablespoon	= 15 mL
2 tablespoons	= 30 mL
1/4 cup	= 60 mL
1/3 cup	= 75 mL
1/2 cup	= 125 mL
2/3 cup	= 150 mL
3/4 cup	= 175 mL
1 cup	= 250 mL
2 cups = 1 pint	= 500 mL
3 cups	= 750 mL
4 cups = 1 quart	= 1 L

VOLUME MEASUREMENTS (fluid)

1 fluid ounce (2 tablespoons)	= 30 mL
4 fluid ounces (1/2 cup)	= 125 mL
8 fluid ounces (1 cup)	= 250 mL
12 fluid ounces (1 1/2 cups)	= 375 mL
16 fluid ounces (2 cups)	= 500 mL

WEIGHTS (mass)

1/2 ounce	= 15 g
1 ounce	= 30 g
3 ounces	= 90 g
4 ounces	= 120 g
8 ounces	= 225 g
10 ounces	= 285 g
12 ounces	= 360 g
16 ounces = 1 pound	= 450 g

DIMENSIONS

1/16 inch	= 2 mm
1/8 inch	= 3 mm
1/4 inch	= 6 mm
1/2 inch	= 1.5 cm
3/4 inch	= 2 cm
1 inch	= 2.5 cm

OVEN TEMPERATURES

250°F	= 120°C
275°F	= 140°C
300°F	= 150°C
325°F	= 160°C
350°F	= 180°C
375°F	= 190°C
400°F	= 200°C
425°F	= 220°C
450°F	= 230°C

BAKING PAN SIZES

Utensil	Size in Inches/Quarts	Metric Volume	Size in Centimeters
Baking or	8×8×2	2 L	20×20×5
Cake Pan	9×9×2	2.5 L	23×23×5
(square or	12×8×2	3 L	30×20×5
rectangular)	13×9×2	3.5 L	33×23×5
Loaf Pan	8×4×3	1.5 L	20×10×7
	9×5×3	2 L	23×13×7
Round Layer	8×1½	1.2 L	20×4
Cake Pan	9×1½	1.5 L	23×4
Pie Plate	8×1¼	750 mL	20×3
	9×1¼	1 L	23×3
Baking Dish	1 quart	1 L	—
or Casserole	1½ quart	1.5 L	—
	2 quart	2 L	—